POCKET
prayers
for GRADUATES

POCKET
prayers
for GRADUATES

40 SIMPLE PRAYERS
THAT BRING HOPE AND DIRECTION

MAX LUCADO

WITH ANDREA LUCADO

THOMAS NELSON
Since 1798

Published in Nashville, Tennessee, by Thomas Nelson. Thomas Nelson is a registered trademark of HarperCollins Christian Publishing, Inc.

Thomas Nelson titles may be purchased in bulk for educational, business, fund-raising, or sales promotional use. For information, please e-mail SpecialMarkets@ThomasNelson.com.

Unless otherwise noted, Scripture quotations are taken from the New King James Version®. © 1982 by Thomas Nelson. Used by permission. All rights reserved.

Scripture quotations marked ESV are from the ESV® Bible (The Holy Bible, English Standard Version®). Copyright © 2001 by Crossway, a publishing ministry of Good News Publishers. Used by permission. All rights reserved.

Scripture quotations marked NCV are from the New Century Version®. © 2005 by Thomas Nelson. Used by permission. All rights reserved.

Scripture quotations marked NIV are from the Holy Bible, New International Version®, NIV®. Copyright © 1973, 1978, 1984, 2011 by Biblica, Inc.® Used by permission of Zondervan. All rights reserved worldwide. www.zondervan.com. The "NIV" and "New International Version" are trademarks registered in the United States Patent and Trademark Office by Biblica, Inc.®

Scripture quotations marked NLT are from the *Holy Bible*, New Living Translation. © 1996, 2004, 2007, 2013 by Tyndale House Foundation. Used by permission of Tyndale House Publishers, Inc., Carol Stream, Illinois 60188. All rights reserved.

Any Internet addresses, phone numbers, or company or product information printed in this book are offered as a resource and are not intended in any way to be or to imply an endorsement by Thomas Nelson, nor does Thomas Nelson vouch for the existence, content, or services of these sites, phone numbers, companies, or products beyond the life of this book.

ISBN 978-0-7180-7833-1 (eBook)

Library of Congress Control Number: 2015956799
ISBN 978-0-7180-7737-2

Printed in Malaysia

23   RRDA   10 9 8 7 6

The Pocket Prayer

Hello, my name is Max. I'm a recovering prayer wimp. I doze off when I pray. My thoughts zig, then zag, then zig again. Distractions swarm like gnats on a summer night. If attention deficit disorder applies to prayer, I am afflicted. When I pray, I think of a thousand things I need to do. I forget the one thing I set out to do: pray.

Some people excel in prayer. They inhale heaven and exhale God. They are the SEAL Team Six of intercession. They would rather pray than sleep. Why is it that I sleep when I pray? They belong to the PGA: Prayer Giants Association. I am a card-carrying member of the PWA: Prayer Wimps Anonymous.

(5)

Can you relate? It's not that we don't pray at all. We all pray some.

On tearstained pillows we pray.

In grand liturgies we pray.

At the sight of geese in flight, we pray.

Quoting ancient devotions, we pray.

We pray to stay sober, centered, or solvent. We pray when the lump is deemed malignant. When the money runs out before the month does. When the unborn baby hasn't kicked in a while. We all pray . . . some.

But wouldn't we all like to pray . . .

More?

Better?

Deeper?

Stronger?

With more fire, faith, or fervency?

Yet we have kids to feed, bills to pay, deadlines to meet.

The calendar pounces on our good intentions like a tiger on a rabbit. We want to pray, but *when*?

We want to pray, but *why*? We might as well admit it. Prayer is odd, peculiar. Speaking into space. Lifting words into the sky. We can't even get the cable company to answer us, yet God will? The doctor is too busy, but God isn't? We have our doubts about prayer.

And we have our checkered history with prayer: unmet expectations, unanswered requests. We can barely genuflect for the scar tissue on our knees. God, to some, is the ultimate heartbreaker. Why keep tossing the coins of our longings into a silent pool? He jilted me once . . . but not twice.

Oh, the peculiar puzzle of prayer.

We aren't the first to struggle. The sign-up sheet for Prayer 101 contains some familiar names: the apostles John, James, Andrew, and Peter. When one of Jesus' disciples requested, "Lord, teach us to pray" (Luke 11:1 NIV), none of the others objected. No one walked away saying, "Hey, I have prayer figured out." The first followers of Jesus needed prayer guidance.

The first followers of Jesus needed prayer guidance.

In fact, the only tutorial they ever requested was on prayer. They could have asked for instructions on many topics: bread multiplying, speech making, storm stilling. Jesus raised people from the dead. But a "How to Vacate the Cemetery" seminar? His followers never called for one. But they did want him to do this: "Lord, teach us to pray."

Might their interest have had something to do with the jaw-dropping, eye-popping promises Jesus attached to prayer? "Ask and it will be given to you" (Matt. 7:7 NIV). "If you believe, you will get anything you ask for in prayer" (Matt. 21:22 NCV). Jesus never attached such power to other endeavors. "*Plan* and it will be given to you." "You will get anything you *work* for." Those words are not in the Bible. But these are—"If you remain in me and follow my teachings, you can ask anything you want, and it will be given to you" (John 15:7 NCV).

Jesus gave stunning prayer promises.

And he set a compelling prayer example. Jesus prayed before he ate. He prayed for children. He prayed for the sick. He prayed with thanks. He prayed with tears. He had made the planets and shaped the stars, yet he prayed. He is the Lord of angels and Commander of heavenly hosts, yet he prayed. He is coequal with God, the exact representation of the Holy One, and yet he devoted himself to prayer. He prayed in the desert, cemetery, and garden. "He went out and departed to a solitary place; and there He prayed" (Mark 1:35).

This dialogue must have been common among his friends:

"Has anyone seen Jesus?"

"Oh, you know. He's up to the same thing."

"Praying *again*?"

"Yep. He's been gone since sunrise."

Jesus would even disappear for an entire night of prayer. I'm thinking of one occasion in particular. He'd just experienced one of the most stressful days of his ministry. The day began with the news of the death of his relative John the Baptist. Jesus sought to retreat with his disciples, yet a throng of thousands followed him. Though grief-stricken, he spent the day teaching and healing people. When it was discovered that the host of people had no food to eat, Jesus multiplied bread out of a basket and fed the entire multitude. In the span of a few hours, he battled sorrow, stress, demands, and needs. He deserved a good night's rest. Yet when evening finally came, he told the crowd to leave and the disciples to board their boat, and "he went up into the hills by himself to pray" (Mark 6:46 NLT).

Apparently it was the correct choice. A storm exploded over the Sea of Galilee, leaving the disciples "in trouble far away from land, for a strong wind had risen, and they were fighting heavy waves. About three o'clock in the morning Jesus came toward them, walking on the water" (Matt. 14:24–25 NLT). Jesus ascended the mountain depleted. He reappeared invigorated. When he reached the water, he never broke his stride. You'd have thought the water was a park lawn and the storm a spring breeze.

Do you think the disciples made the prayer–power connection? "Lord, teach us to pray *like that*. Teach us to find strength in prayer. To banish fear in prayer. To defy storms in prayer. To come off the mountain of prayer with the authority of a prince."

What about you? The disciples faced angry waves and a watery grave. You face angry clients, a turbulent economy, raging seas of stress and sorrow.

"Lord," we still request, "teach us to pray."

When the disciples asked Jesus to teach them to pray, he gave them a prayer. Not a lecture on prayer. Not the doctrine of prayer. He gave them a quotable, repeatable, portable prayer (Luke 11:1–4).

Could you use the same? It seems to me that the prayers of the Bible can be distilled into one. The result is a simple, easy-to-remember, pocket-size prayer:

Father,

> *you are good.*
>> *I need help. Heal me and forgive me.*
>>> *They need help.*
>>>> *Thank you.*
>>>>> *In Jesus' name, amen.*

Let this prayer punctuate your day. As you begin your morning, *Father, you are good.* As you commute to work or walk the hallways at school, *I need help.* As you wait in the grocery line, *They need help.* Keep this prayer in your pocket as you pass through the day.

When we invite God into our world, he walks in. He brings

a host of gifts: joy, patience, resilience. Anxieties come, but they don't stick. Fears surface and then depart. Regrets land on the windshield, but then comes the wiper of prayer. The devil still hands me stones of guilt, but I turn and give them to Christ. I'm completing my sixth decade, yet I'm wired with energy. I am happier, healthier, and more hopeful than I have ever been. Struggles come, for sure. But so does God.

Prayer is not a privilege for the pious, not the art of a chosen few. Prayer is simply a heartfelt conversation between God and his child.

Prayer is not a privilege for the pious, not the art of a chosen few. Prayer is simply a heartfelt conversation between God and his child. My friend, he wants to talk with you. Even now, as you read these words, he taps at the door. Open it. Welcome him in. Let the conversation begin.

Prayers for My Relationship with God

1

I am the vine, you are the branches. He who abides in Me, and I in him, bears much fruit; for without Me you can do nothing.

JOHN 15:5

Dear God, without you I am nothing. Without you I can't do anything. You are my everything—my strength, my joy, and my comfort.

Teach me what it means to abide in you. Strengthen my relationship with you. Bring me closer to you so I will walk with you every day and get to know you more and more.

I pray for my family. I feel too far away to help them, but I know you are with them, and I know they trust you.

Thank you that we get to have a relationship with you, our God.

In Jesus' name, amen.

2

He who walks with wise men will be wise, but the companion of fools will be destroyed.

PROVERBS 13:20

Dear Father, you sent your Son, Jesus, to establish your church here on earth. You did not leave us alone, because you care about us so much.

Help me find a church and a group of other Christians in this new school and in this new place. Let it be a place that is safe, and let there be wise mentors to help guide me.

I pray for the leaders in my new church. Guide the pastors, ministers, and elders, and give them your wisdom.

Thank you for your church.

In Jesus' name I pray, amen.

3

---

*And these words which I command you today
shall be in your heart. You shall teach them
diligently to your children, and shall talk of them
when you sit in your house, when you walk by the
way, when you lie down, and when you rise up.*

DEUTERONOMY 6:6-7

Father, your law is love, and your love is so strong I cannot understand it. You love your creation and everything that is in it.

Lord, remind me of your words when I wake up in the morning, when I go to sleep at night, and as I go about my day-to-day life. Write your words on my heart.

Help my family and friends at home, the ones who taught me about you and your love for me. Stay close to them, and remind them of your promises today.

Thank you for giving me your Word, which helps me know you better.

In Jesus' name, amen.

4

And let us consider one another in order to stir up love and good works, not forsaking the assembling of ourselves together, as is the manner of some, but exhorting one another, and so much the more as you see the Day approaching.

HEBREWS 10:24-25

Dear God, you are so faithful. You are so good to me, your child. Everything you do is righteous and for your glory.

I need help finding a Christian community. Would you put people in my life who will encourage me, and help me encourage others?

I pray for the people who do ministry in this town and on this campus. I pray that they will feel strengthened by those around them.

Thank you that we are never alone in our Christian walk.

In Christ I pray, amen.

5

For My flesh is food indeed, and My blood is drink indeed. He who eats My flesh and drinks My blood abides in Me, and I in him. As the living Father sent Me, and I live because of the Father, so he who feeds on Me will live because of Me. This is the bread which came down from heaven— not as your fathers ate the manna, and are dead. He who eats this bread will live forever.

JOHN 6:55-58

Dear God, you really are all that I need. You are the answer to all my questions. You are my hope when I feel hopeless.

Please forgive me for looking to other people and other things to fulfill me or make me happy. I want to serve only you. Bring me back to you, God.

Help my friends who are not following you right now but have started going after empty, worldly things. Remind them that you are what they need.

I am so grateful you are my God and my Father.

In Jesus' name, amen.

6

As iron sharpens iron, so a man sharpens
the countenance of his friend.

PROVERBS 27:17

Dear God, you are a wise and good Father. My relationship with you is the most important relationship in my life.

I ask for your wisdom today, God. I need it more than ever now that I have graduated and am on my own. Give me wise friends who love you and will encourage my relationship with you.

I pray for my friends who are in the same phase of life as I am. Please bring mentors to encourage them along the way.

Thank you for being so close to me during this time.

In Jesus' holy name, amen.

7

Then Jesus said to those Jews who believed Him, "If you abide in My word, you are My disciples indeed. And you shall know the truth, and the truth shall make you free."

JOHN 8:31-32

Dear God, your Word is true. It is powerful and life changing.

Please give me more passion for your Word. I get so busy that I don't take the time to read my Bible. Help me to set aside time each day to read at least a few verses. I know that can change my life and my heart.

Be with those people who don't have Bibles in their homes or even in their country. Take them your Word through other ways, and change their hearts with it.

Thank you for giving us your Word, which is true every day.

In Christ's name, amen.

Prayers for My Future

8

---

*Trust in the L*ORD *with all your heart, and*
lean not on your own understanding;
in all your ways acknowledge Him,
and He shall direct your paths.

PROVERBS 3:5-6

Father, you direct my path. You know everything about my future, and you care about me.

Today I feel overwhelmed by decisions I need to make. I'm not sure which way to go, and it feels like too much to handle. Show me the best choice in every situation.

Be with my family today. Show them that they can trust you no matter how hard or confusing life is right now.

Thank you for being a good Father I can trust each day. Thank you for listening to me.

In Jesus' name, amen.

9

If any of you lacks wisdom, let him ask of God, who gives to all liberally and without reproach, and it will be given to him.

JAMES 1:5

Dear God, you are wise, loving, and generous. You don't hold back any good thing from me or any of your children.

I ask for wisdom in this new season of life. Guide me as I walk through my day, meet new people, and have new experiences. Make me wiser as I get to know you better.

Be with my friends who are starting new schools and new jobs. When situations arise, help them ask you, before anyone else, what they should do so they will make wise decisions.

I'm grateful for these new opportunities to grow and to learn.

In Christ I pray, amen.

10

For I know the thoughts that I think toward you, says the LORD, thoughts of peace and not of evil, to give you a future and a hope.

JEREMIAH 29:11

Dear Father, you are the God of hope. You are the God of my past, present, and future.

Sometimes things are confusing and hard. Right now it's hard for me to believe I have a bright future. Help me have hope, and show me the good things you have planned for me.

Comfort my friends and those in my family who feel lost. Bring them peace when they feel restless, and bring them hope when they feel discouraged and alone.

Thank you for your plan for me even though I don't yet know what it is.

In Jesus' name, amen.

11

Now this is the confidence that we have in Him, that if we ask anything according to His will, He hears us. And if we know that He hears us, whatever we ask, we know that we have the petitions that we have asked of Him.

1 JOHN 5:14-15

God, you hear all my prayers. You are kind, understanding, and faithful. You never get tired of listening to me.

Father, help me understand what next step I should take with my work and education. Show me when I read my Bible. Show me when I talk to wise friends and mentors. I know you answer when I ask.

I have friends who are angry because they didn't get what they prayed for. Help them feel your love for them, and remind them that you always hear their prayers—even when your plans are different than theirs.

Thank you for answered and unanswered prayers.

It's in Jesus' name I pray, amen.

12

Your ears shall hear a word behind you,
saying, "This is the way, walk in it,"
whenever you turn to the right hand
or whenever you turn to the left.

ISAIAH 30:21

Good Father, you are the same God today as the God I read about in the Bible. You never change.

I hear so many voices in my head telling me what to do next with my life that I don't know which one to trust. Help me know which voice is yours, the only trustworthy voice.

Give my friends the courage to do what you are asking of them. It is tempting to go in the wrong direction, but what you have planned for them is best.

Thank you for being with me during this time of change and for promising that you will be with me forever.

In Jesus' name, amen.

13

*But the wisdom that is from above is first
pure, then peaceable, gentle, willing to
yield, full of mercy and good fruits.*

JAMES 3:17

Dear God, every gift from you is perfect. There is nothing bad in you. You never make mistakes.

Let this year be my chance to start over. Let it be the year I begin to follow you, really follow you. And let my life show the fruit of the Spirit to those around me.

Help my parents. Give them a sense of your presence and the strength to keep leading our family, and don't let them get discouraged.

Thank you for caring for each member of my family.

In Christ I pray, amen.

14

Listen to counsel and receive instruction, that you may be wise in your latter days. There are many plans in a man's heart, nevertheless the LORD's counsel—that will stand.

PROVERBS 19:20-21

Father, your Word will last forever. Everything you say is true and full of love.

I need forgiveness for following my own plans. In school I often got sidetracked thinking about what I wanted instead of what you want. Now I want only to do your will. Help me know what it is.

Many of my friends feel helpless right now because they can't find jobs, and they're not sure what to do next. Give them unexpected opportunities, and give them hope.

Thank you for your forgiveness and your faithfulness.

In Christ's name, amen.

Prayers for Strength and Conviction

15

Fight the good fight of faith, lay hold on eternal life, to which you were also called and have confessed the good confession in the presence of many witnesses. I urge you in the sight of God who gives life to all things, and before Christ Jesus who witnessed the good confession before Pontius Pilate, that you keep this commandment without spot, blameless until our Lord Jesus Christ's appearing.

1 TIMOTHY 6:12–14

Father, you are fighting for me. You won the war over sin, and now you reign in my heart as the King of my life.

I'm having trouble keeping my eyes on you. Some people I've met at school pressure me to do things I don't want to do, and it's hard to say no. Keep me focused on you and the purpose you have for me.

Please help my Christian friends at other schools to "fight the good fight of faith." Don't let them get distracted, but help them stand strong in your Word.

Thank you for being the Rock I can stand on.

In Jesus' name, amen.

16

Therefore submit to God. Resist the devil and he will flee from you. Draw near to God and He will draw near to you.

JAMES 4:7-8

Dear God, you are the creator of everything beautiful in the world, including the mountains, oceans, rivers, and seasons. And yet you want to have a relationship with me, your child.

Draw near to me, God. Be close to me so I don't stumble into sin. It is easy to do that here, in a new place with new people.

I'm worried about people in my family who are not following you and don't seem to have much faith. Please remind them today of your love.

Thank you for sending your Son so we can always be near you.

In Jesus' name, amen.

17

Stand therefore, having girded your waist
with truth, having put on the breastplate of
righteousness, and having shod your feet with
the preparation of the gospel of peace; above all,
taking the shield of faith with which you will be
able to quench all the fiery darts of the wicked
one. And take the helmet of salvation, and the
sword of the Spirit, which is the word of God.

EPHESIANS 6:14-17

Father, you are truth, righteousness, and peace. With you, anything is possible. No problem is too big for you to solve.

In my job, I sometimes have a hard time standing up for what I believe. No one around me seems to care about you. Strengthen me each day before I go to work to live in your truth.

Be with my coworkers today. Help them see who you are by the way I and other Christians act around them.

Thank you for this job and for being with me no matter where I am.

In Christ's name I pray, amen.

18

Do not be conformed to this world, but be
transformed by the renewing of your mind,
that you may prove what is that good and
acceptable and perfect will of God.

ROMANS 12:2

Dear God, you are holy and deserve all the glory.

Sometimes I feel unsure about my beliefs because of the influences around me. Give me confidence in my faith, Lord. I don't want to be like the world. I want to be like Jesus.

I pray for our church leaders. When people come to them with doubts and questions, please give them the words to say, and encourage them.

Thank you for my church and the people who taught me to love and believe in you.

In Jesus' name, amen.

19

---

*For am I now seeking the approval of man,
or of God? . . . If I were still trying to please
man, I would not be a servant of Christ.*

GALATIANS 1:10 ESV

Dear Father, you are always the same. No matter what I do or say, your love never changes.

Forgive me for the times I have been embarrassed about my Christian faith. I want people to like me so badly sometimes, but I know you are the only person I need to please, and I know you care about me.

Please give me the courage to speak up for you, to be bold in faith, kind in speech, and thoughtful in actions.

Thank you for the blessings in my life. There are so many.

In Jesus' name, amen.

20

---

*For those who live according to the flesh set
their minds on the things of the flesh, but those
who live according to the Spirit, the things of
the Spirit. For to be carnally minded is death,
but to be spiritually minded is life and peace.*

ROMANS 8:5-6

God, you give me grace every day. You never run out. I can count on your grace for the rest of my life.

As life gets busier and more difficult, it's easy to concentrate on things that discourage me or bring me down. Help me focus on everything that is peaceful and good and life giving.

I pray that my friends and family find hope and peace when they read your Word today. Let them read something that sticks with them and helps them.

Thank you for giving me peace and comfort during this new time in my life.

In Christ I pray, amen.

21

Do not forget my law, but let your heart keep my commands; for length of days and long life and peace they will add to you. Let not mercy and truth forsake you; bind them around your neck, write them on the tablet of your heart.

PROVERBS 3:1-3

Dear God, you are the only judge. You are the only One who knows my heart through and through.

I am learning so many new things in life and in class. But don't let me forget what you have taught me and what I learned in church. Write your law on my heart so I will always remember it.

I pray for my teachers and classmates who don't believe in you. Show them who you are and how much you love and care for them.

Thank you for bringing me to this place to learn new things about you and your creation.

In Jesus' name, amen.

Prayers for Hope
and Peace

22

The end of a thing is better than its beginning... Do not say, "Why were the former days better than these?" For you do not inquire wisely concerning this. Wisdom is good with an inheritance, and profitable to those who see the sun.

ECCLESIASTES 7:8, 10-11

Father, you are the beginning and the end. You live outside of time, and you know ahead of time everything that will happen.

I feel sad today and need your comfort. I know graduation is an exciting time, but it is also bittersweet to say good-bye to family and friends. Give me joy and excitement in this time of change.

Some of my friends aren't leaving home, and I know it is hard for them to watch everybody else move on and go different places. Help them know you have a special plan and purpose for them too.

Thank you for new beginnings.

In Jesus' name, amen.

23

---

*To everything there is a season, a time
for every purpose under heaven: a time
to be born, and a time to die; . . . a time to
break down, and a time to build up.*

ECCLESIASTES 3:1-3

Dear God, your timing is perfect. You don't let anything happen too late or too early.

But I don't feel ready for this next step in life. I'm afraid because I don't know what's ahead of me. Give me the confidence I need just for today.

Be with my family, who is also affected by this transition. Be a rock for all of us, and let them lean on you for whatever they need.

Thank you that everything in my life can be used for your purposes.

In Christ I pray, amen.

24

One thing I do: Forgetting what is behind and straining toward what is ahead, I press on toward the goal to win the prize for which God has called me heavenward in Christ Jesus.

PHILIPPIANS 3:13-14 NIV

Dear Father, you forgive and forget all my sins. You are the reason I can live without regret.

Lord, I have so many what-if questions right now. Moving forward is hard when I have questions about my past. Give me the courage to press on toward the goal and not look back.

Be close to my friends who are hard on themselves about their pasts. Teach them what forgiveness is so they can be free.

Thank you for Christ, who has set us free.

In his name I pray, amen.

25

Do not remember the former things, nor consider the things of old. Behold, I will do a new thing, now it shall spring forth; shall you not know it? I will even make a road in the wilderness and rivers in the desert.

ISAIAH 43:18-19

God, you make the impossible possible. You can create a river in the middle of a desert, and you make good things happen when I least expect them.

It's hard for me to imagine life being better than it is now. You brought me so many blessings these last few years, and I've come a long way with you beside me. Stay close to me as I take the next step.

Some of my friends have had a difficult few years. Please give them hope for their future. Give them a river in the middle of their desert.

Thank you for the hope we have in you.

In Jesus' name, amen.

26

The Lord is my shepherd; I shall not want.
He makes me to lie down in green pastures;
He leads me beside the still waters. He
restores my soul; He leads me in the paths
of righteousness for His name's sake.

PSALM 23:1-3

Father, you are a good shepherd to your people. You know each one of us, and when we get lost, you come and find us.

Remind me of this again and again today: "He leads me in the paths of righteousness." When I'm not sure where my life is going or what changes are ahead, show me the right path and bring me peace.

Comfort my friends who are going through some hard changes. As your Word says, lead them beside still waters and restore their souls.

Thank you for leading me with love.

In Christ's name I pray, amen.

27

Be anxious for nothing, but in everything by prayer and supplication, with thanksgiving, let your requests be made known to God; and the peace of God, which surpasses all understanding, will guard your hearts and minds through Christ Jesus.

PHILIPPIANS 4:6-7

G od, you protect my heart and my mind. You bring me perfect peace whenever I ask for it.

I am anxious today, Father. Life is exciting but scary right now. A good chapter has closed, and now I begin a new job with new people. Give me the kind of peace that only you can give.

I pray right now for all the new students at my school. I remember how scary it was to start a new year. Protect them from anxious thoughts.

Thank you for the opportunity to try new things in life.

In Jesus' name, amen.

28

---

*Have I not commanded you? Be strong
and of good courage; do not be afraid,
nor be dismayed, for the LORD your
God is with you wherever you go.*

JOSHUA 1:9

Father, you are faithful. You never leave me. Wherever I am, you are there too.

God, help me be strong, and help me have courage. Don't let worry get in the way of my being joyful and excited about this fresh start.

Be with my family wherever they go. Even though we are not together as much now, remind them that you are always with them.

Thank you for your presence in my life every day.

In your name I pray, amen.

Prayers for My Work and Career

29

And whatever you do, do it heartily, as to the Lord and not to men, knowing that from the Lord you will receive the reward of the inheritance; for you serve the Lord Christ.

COLOSSIANS 3:23-24

Dear God, you are the reason for everything I do. Without you, I have no purpose.

Sometimes I get caught up in work and in wanting to please my boss and the people around me. Change my heart, God. Help me want to please you first, because your opinion is all that matters. I'll never be able to please everyone else.

I pray for my boss and the other supervisors at work. Take away the pressure they feel, and help them lean on you.

Thank you for being with me at work even when I'm not focused on you.

In Jesus' name, amen.

30

I have shown you in every way, by laboring like this, that you must support the weak. And remember the words of the Lord Jesus, that He said, "It is more blessed to give than to receive."

ACTS 20:35

Dear God, you gave us the best gift of all: your Son. You sacrificed everything to be near us.

Forgive me for getting so worried about my job that I forget to serve the people around me—my coworkers, family, friends, and people who have less than I do. Give me a servant heart, which is more important than any job title I could ever have.

Be close to those who don't have much today, who don't have a home or a family or work to do. Help them realize they are your children and are important in your eyes.

Thank you for looking out for each one of your children.

In Jesus' name, amen.

31

Let your light so shine before men,
that they may see your good works
and glorify your Father in heaven.

MATTHEW 5:16

Father, you are everywhere all the time. Even in my darkest moments you shine through, and I can see you.

God, help me be a light today in my workplace. I feel as if I'm the only one here who knows you, and it's hard to keep following you. Help me stand up for you, no matter what, so you will be glorified.

I want my coworkers to know you. Work on their hearts. Give them a desire to learn about you and the Bible. Show them how much you love them.

Thank you for the people I've met during this new experience.

In your name I pray, amen.

32

Remind them to be subject to rulers and authorities, to obey, to be ready for every good work, to speak evil of no one, to be peaceable, gentle, showing all humility to all men.

TITUS 3:1-2

Dear Father, you are a good ruler. You are fair, and you want justice. I can trust in your good judgment.

Humble me today. I am struggling with authority in my life and at work. It's hard for me to follow a leader I don't respect or trust. Give me wisdom, and help me let go of this situation and give it to you to handle.

I pray for the people you have placed in authority over me. Show them how to lead with kindness and courage.

Thank you for caring about every detail of my life.

In Jesus' name, amen.

33

Repay no one evil for evil. Have regard for good things in the sight of all men. If it is possible, as much as depends on you, live peaceably with all men. Beloved, do not avenge yourselves, but rather give place to wrath; for it is written, "Vengeance is Mine, I will repay," says the Lord.

Romans 12:17-19

D ear God, you are sovereign. Nothing happens that you don't know about or care about. You see it all.

I need your peace right now. I feel that I've been wronged and blamed for things I haven't done, and I'm afraid I'll lose the respect of friends and coworkers. I surrender this situation to you. I know that you're the final judge and that you want good things for my life.

Be with my family during this time. Give them hope and faith in you and in me. Make them stronger, and give them joy in the middle of the stressful times.

Thank you for your mercies and your promises.

In Jesus' name, amen.

34

My beloved brethren, be steadfast, immovable, always abounding in the work of the Lord, knowing that your labor is not in vain in the Lord.

1 Corinthians 15:58

God, you can redeem anything. You can turn around even the worst situation and make it better than I could imagine.

Give me hope in my job. It's not exactly what I thought it would be, and I don't always feel motivated and excited by it. Remind me that anything I do is for you, so I should do it with all my heart. Remind me often that this is the first step on a new life path.

I have friends who don't love their jobs right now. Remind them to work joyfully because you love them, not because they have their dream jobs.

I am so grateful your plan is better than mine.

In Christ I pray, amen.

35

And He said to me, "My grace is sufficient for you, for My strength is made perfect in weakness." Therefore most gladly I will rather boast in my infirmities, that the power of Christ may rest upon me.

2 Corinthians 12:9

God, you really are all that I need. Your grace is sufficient for me.

In this new job I often feel as though I don't know what I'm doing. I'm afraid of failing. But, Lord, I know that your strength is made perfect in my weakness, so please be my strength today.

Some of my family members need to be reminded of your grace. They work so hard, but it never feels like enough. Show them your grace—a gift they don't have to earn.

Thank you for your grace and your strength, which lift me up.

In your name, amen.

Prayers for Relationships

36

*Two are better than one, because they have
a good reward for their labor. For if they
fall, one will lift up his companion.*

ECCLESIASTES 4:9-10

Father, you did not create us to be alone. You are with me. The Holy Spirit is with me, and you have given me friends and family who bless me.

But today I feel lonely. This city is new, and I want friends and someone I can depend on to help me when I fall. Please bring people like that into my life.

Show me the people around me, who are also lonely, that I could befriend. Give them the hope and godly confidence they need to meet new people.

Thank you for always hearing my prayers.

In Jesus' name, amen.

37

A new commandment I give to you, that you love one another; as I have loved you, that you also love one another. By this all will know that you are My disciples, if you have love for one another.

JOHN 13:34-35

Dear God, you are love. I know this because your Word says so, and I know this because I know that you love me so much.

Help me love other people the way you love them. When a new relationship starts for me, don't let me get caught up in what the world says is love. Teach me what real love is.

Show your love to the people in my life. Fill them up with it until your love is all they need.

Thank you for loving us no matter where we come from, who we are, or what we do.

In Jesus' name, amen.

38

---

*Walk worthy of the calling with which
you were called, with all lowliness and
gentleness, with longsuffering, bearing with
one another in love, endeavoring to keep
the unity of the Spirit in the bond of peace.*

EPHESIANS 4:1-3

Father, you sent your Son to serve us here on earth even though we didn't deserve it. But you loved us so much you did it anyway.

Forgive me for my selfishness, especially in my relationships with friends and loved ones. I think about me most of the time, but help me think about you and others first.

I know so many wonderful servant-hearted people. Please give them the encouragement and energy they need to keep serving and loving people.

Thank you for these good examples you have put in my life.

In Christ I pray, amen.

39

Children, obey your parents in the Lord, for this is right. "Honor your father and mother," which is the first commandment with promise: "that it may be well with you and you may live long on the earth."

Ephesians 6:1-3

Dear Father, you can fix anything that is broken. Nothing and no one is unfixable for you. You are bigger than our pain and our problems.

Lord, it has been hard for me to get along with my parents and family in this phase of life. I feel independent, but they don't see me that way. Show me how to honor you and my parents.

Give my parents the courage to let go. When they are holding on to me and my siblings too much, replace their fear with peace, and comfort them during this time of change.

Thank you for giving us courage and strength.

In Jesus' name, amen.

40

---

*For God did not appoint us to wrath, but
to obtain salvation through our Lord Jesus
Christ, who died for us, that whether we
wake or sleep, we should live together with
Him. Therefore comfort each other and edify
one another, just as you also are doing.*

1 Thessalonians 5:9-11

Father, my relationship with you is the most important one in my life. You matter more than anyone or anything else.

But I am tempted to put my relationships with others before you, God. Forgive me for doing that, and remind me to put you first in my life always.

Encourage my loved ones today. Show them how to prioritize their relationships and their time. Give them a desire for you above anything and anyone else.

Thank you for creating me and wanting a relationship with me.

It's in your name I pray, amen.

About Max Lucado

More than 120 million readers have found inspiration and encouragement in the writings of Max Lucado. He lives with his wife, Denalyn, and their mischievous mutt, Andy, in San Antonio, Texas, where he serves the people of Oak Hills Church. Visit his website at MaxLucado.com or follow him at Twitter.com/MaxLucado and Facebook.com/MaxLucado.

About Andrea Lucado

Andrea Lucado is a freelance writer and Texas native who now calls Nashville, Tennessee, home. When she is not conducting interviews or writing stories, you can find her laughing with friends at a coffee shop, running the hills of Nashville or creating yet another nearly edible baking creation in her kitchen. One of these days she'll get the recipe right. Follow her on Twitter and Instagram, @andrealucado, or on her blog at AndreaLucado.com.

Discover Even More Power in a Simple Prayer

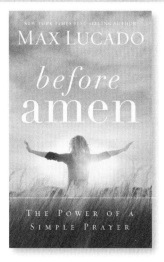

ISBN 978-0-7180-7812-6
$15.99

Join Max Lucado on a journey to the very heart of biblical prayer and discover rest in the midst of chaos and confidence even for prayer wimps.

Available wherever books are sold.

BeforeAmen.com

Make Your Prayers Personal

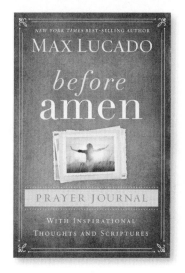

ISBN 978-0-7180-1406-3

$13.99

This beautiful companion journal to *Before Amen* helps readers stoke their prayer life. It features quotes and scriptures to inspire both prayer warriors and those who struggle to pray.

Tools for Your Church and Small Group

Before Amen: A DVD Study

ISBN 978-0-529-12342-8

$21.99

Max Lucado leads this four-session study through his discovery of a simple tool for connecting with God each day. This study will help small-group participants build their prayer life, calm the chaos of their world, and grow in Christ.

Before Amen Study Guide

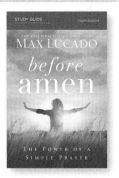

ISBN 978-0-529-12334-3

$9.99

This guide is filled with Scripture study, discussion questions, and practical ideas designed to help small-group members understand Jesus' teaching on prayer. An integral part of the *Before Amen* small-group study, it will help group members build prayer into their everyday lives.

Before Amen
Church Campaign Kit

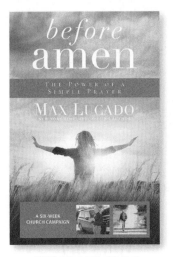

ISBN 978-0-529-12369-5

$49.99

The church campaign kit includes a four-session DVD study by Max Lucado; a study guide with discussion questions and video notes; the *Before Amen* trade book; a getting started guide; and access to a website with all the sermon resources churches need to launch and sustain a four-week *Before Amen* campaign.

Before Amen for Everyone

Before Amen Audiobook

ISBN 978-1-4915-4662-8 | $19.99

Enjoy the unabridged audio CD of *Before Amen*.

Before Amen eBook

ISBN 978-0-529-12390-9

Read *Before Amen* anywhere on your
favorite tablet or electronic device.

Antes del amén Spanish Edition

ISBN 978-0-7180-0157-5 | $13.99

The hope of *Before Amen* is also available for
Spanish-language readers.